Dozens

OTHER POETRY BY DAVID R. SLAVITT

Dozens

A POEM BY DAVID R. SLAVITT

Louisiana State University Press
BATON ROUGE AND LONDON   1981

IN MEMORY OF MY FATHER

Copyright © 1981 by David R. Slavitt
All rights reserved
Manufactured in the United States of America

Designer: Joanna Hill
Typeface: Trump Medieval
Typesetter: G & S Typesetters, Inc.
Printer: Thomson-Shore, Inc.
Binder: John Dekker and Sons

LIBRARY OF CONGRESS CATALOGING IN PUBLICATION DATA

Slavitt, David R   1935–
    Dozens : a poem.

    I. Title.
PS3569.L3D6   811'.54   80-24330
ISBN 0-8071-0787-5
ISBN 0-8071-0788-3 pbk.

Only it requires a skill in the varying of the serenade that occasionally makes me feel like a Guatemalan when one particularly wants to feel like an Italian.

Wallace Stevens, letter to
Harriet Monroe

Dozens

1.

Admitting that I am lost, that my calculations
have brought me round again to the same spot
or a spot that looks the same, the light, the shadows
the same, and the trees, scrub pines looking
all alike, I must make a different
plan, boldly silly. I'll do what
the sheriff does, holding in front of his hound's
snout some object, a garment, give it a sniff
of the thing's tang, and let it go, let it
quarter the ground, baying me back, obeying.
Give it its head. If I have to get down on all
fours and be my own hound, rough. Rough.

2.

There was a courtyard. There is still a courtyard.
I've been back, have stood in the pouring rain,
peering at faces, looking for mine or for one
who knows me. Is that old Charlie under the *vaste
portique*? Or old Wally under the huge
portico in this remembered abode,
the habitat of imagination? On these
stones serious drunks have lurched and gray
visitors staggered giddy with freedom. "Of what
is this house composed if not of the sun. . . ?" Stevens
asked. The shield on our gate showed three
suns; dazzled, we thought they had to be rising.

3.

Earlier, glare on snow and paths plowed
crisscross, making the quadrangles envelopes.
Faculty poodles romped in packs to suggest
a settlement of decadent esquimaux.
Not thinking caps, but boots are for intellection.
A snowy page is still a trackless waste
to play in or plow through. This city snow
turns dirty (and melts faster than clean).
But it still can happen. Two or three nights a year
the transformation occurs and the morning sun
dazzles, the snow daggers my eyes with its glitter.
Hoo. Haa. My breath ghosts like a child's.

4.

We know what we need to know. The trick is need,
in having the need, in fast-talking the banker
for a letter of credit. "Yes, indeed, I credit
letters, always try to show interest, don't
want to be no-account . . ." "Owe," the man said,
"a million and you've got yourself a partner."
I'm lightly sketched and yearn to be overdrawn,
but he sees through me, scarcely sees me at all.
I have to raise my voice. He cares nothing for words,
won't risk even a penny for my two cents' worth
(*Tu pense!*) and asks about my deeds.
For close, he throws me out by the seat of my *pense*.

5.

Firbank had his palm; I have a dying
monster with two-foot leaves, of which five
are left, two of them still healthy. My flowering
hawthorne's gone, the Rothschild azalea, the gaudy
bromeliads, the wistaria, all gone,
not dead but abandoned, and mourned the more,
toys confiscated for bad behavior.
My parents' unruly oak sighed my complaints
through summer nights. Its black squirrels were my mavericks.
You were too big for the plot, pal. They're still
hacking you back, to save their windows, to keep you
from mauling pieces of roof off the garage.

6.

I learn to lower my views. The angle of vision
close to the ground is rewarding—a dime, two pennies,
just this week. Those loftier vistas lose
particularity. All objects object
to servitude to Il Grande del Prospettivo,
a fascist older than Benito. They languish,
give up their ghosts. In democratic sunlight
I've seen glints from survivors, pieces of glass,
flecks in the concrete, shining puddles, have glimpsed
a world littered with diamonds, flash-plated silver.
Knowing better is often knowing worse.
Basta! Down with the tyrant! Death to Il Grande!

7.

To go west is to go where the sun dies,
but east is where darkness comes from, is worse. My desk
faces east. Light, in the morning, splashes
the wall behind me. Now it's in front. Each passage
feels like a wave, which makes this the bridge
of a ship, breasting the light, making for port
wherever the heart of darkness is. The pious
pray facing in this direction. The impious
sit, feeling uneasy. Instead of *mincha*
or vespers, when dark comes, I walk the dog.
I jingle the keys. He comes running, jumps,
does a little dance that serves us both as prayer.

8.

"Obviously," says Il Grande, and "inevitably,"
and on lofty occasions (but most of his occasions
are lofty), "inexorably," and we bow
to such suave assurance as we crave ourselves.
The intellectual manner is easy to ape
(the manners of apes, spontaneous, crude, but gentle,
are more demanding). My point is that his point
vanishes, his roads all narrow
to nothing, lead past stunted trees to the tiny
purlieus next to nowhere. Baboons know better
who live only in near trees, big with phenomenal
figs, coconuts, dates, persimmons, bananas.

9.

The barman in the monkey jacket mixes
exotic essences for our jaded palates,
and at the buffet behind their appalling piles
of food, the chefs in tall toques defy us
with abundance to which only newcomers do justice.
The rest here at the Hotel Magnifico
pick and languish, gasp through afternoons
of Fernet-Branca and dread of dinner's affront.
Beyond the gates and those orderly garden vistas,
pythons are said to be hanging in the trees
like animated guts, ravening; their
lively tongues flick-flick in the jacarandas.

10.

The Aporia, Greek owned but with a German
crew and Liberian flag, has broken up
in the sorry straits where wrecks of old galleys
shift with the tides. Mail has been lost, and cargo,
pharmaceuticals, coriander, toys . . .
Imagine the hearty, healthy sharks, eating
our mushrooms *à la grecque* and reading our letters
with their fishy eyes. Il conte is not amused,
leaves the veranda. I wasn't talking to him
but to and for myself (I tell myself).
Until the sun reaches the yardarm what
to do, but pass the time like a kidney stone?

11.

The foliage begins, a green wall,
but it yields like a trick, swallowing up girls,
automobiles, tanks, brigades, roads,
whole towns. Cheetahs lurk, and vipers;
gaudy parrots iterate the "How
about it honey?" they've picked up on their perches
above our cabanas. The only attraction to jungle
is the hotel's dwindling away, behind . . .
another trick that wouldn't work for me.
I'd lug the place along as big as life.
Surprisingly, everything is. The droplet of venom,
spider's, scorpion's, milky or clear, is.

12.

Sister Selena, reader and advisor,
may have the powers she claims, may have them often.
Ignore the cards, the tea leaves. She does, doesn't
use her crystal ball except as a prop,
a sign, as a pharmacist keeps those beakers of green
liquid up on a shelf. She apperceives
her patrons as a bank officer would,
takes them in by hunches and hints as a maître
d'hôtel would. She tells them what they are:
what they fear and what they desire follows.
And what to expect? Look at her face, her hands,
her shoes. Her guess is as good as anyone's.

13.

What poet could set up shop in a storefront,
hang bead curtains, install a few hideous lamps,
and read and advise the troubled, the worried, the restless,
telling them who they are? Some days you have it;
others, you don't. She puts on a good show,
offensive to the ministry of commerce
but tolerated by its own board of tourismo.
Shrewder than poets would be, she pays small bribes
for Coronel Corrupcion's protection.
She smokes too much, sleeps late, plays solitaire
as most of us will, awaiting our occasions.
Her two black cats sing heavenly mews.

14.

If stanzas are rooms, then poems must be buildings,
and volumes, streets, whole towns, impositions
of minds upon topography. A harbor,
a defensible hill may prompt, but the human eye,
full of its own humors, orders the prospect
and fails—one's best vision being blind.
These dodecahedrons then are living rooms
in a random dwelling. I sit in its dark, guessing
what city would least disresemble mine,
what square, what series of shops, what gable,
slick in the streetlit rain, reverberate right
to the footsteps I want to take, or want to have taken.

15.

Snow again. The city staggers, its sidewalks
slick, its roads glassy as a drunk's
eyes. We slide through its delusions, look
for a reasonable footing. Plowblades scrape,
striking sparks of cartoon rage. Trucks
spread salt, sand, and cinders, a formulary
mixture of grit. (The gritty is truth, is fact;
the slick is like our own insides, fantastic,
treacherous, and disgusting.) Even the slums
gleam clean for a while, but emergency crews
are out scattering truths to bring them back
to what they were, and have to be, and are.

16.

Realty is reality; space is to buy
and sell, rent, mortgage if you have to,
fight for if you must. Sovereigns without it
pretend. Citizens w less than 300 sq
ft (2 rms) per capita are squeezed
to drunkenness, madness, and dream states dangerous
to the real *état*. Therefore we fear them
and do not venture at night to their mean demesnes.
Darkness is their ally, destroying space
as any architect will tell you. El Jefe
puts in those mercury vapor lamps, bright lights
that kill trees and dreams but keep streets safe.

17.

Plink, plink, plink. The trees on the plan are seeds
for trees in the world in neat rows to show
scale, to relieve the brutalizing of concrete,
apologizing—as bas relief motifs
of oak and acanthus and ivy leaves used to
acknowledge nature out there somewhere, begging
its gentle blessing or forgiveness. Nature
and art now are fixed percentages
of the cost, the public policy paying lip service
to what no one believes. Each tree has its hole
in the concrete where dogs go, hunched over,
straining to imagine fertile fields.

18.

So Carlos Williams begins, considering
a dog sniffing, considering, a tree
in Paterson. A dreadful city, as Whitman's
Camden is a dreadful city. The worse
it is, the better it is. To live in a foundered
dream is instructive. The squalid moment, blind
as a boarded window, turns the vision inward
or backward to the dead builders' desires
for grace and order. Communal efforts, cities
are cathedrals of our time, never finished,
monuments to the happenstance of what
we are, or wanted, or what has become of us.

19.

The eye glazes; familiarity washes
unlovely alleys, sentimentalizes,
as bad painters would, their random rubble.
The brutest truth turns tame, as that theater wall
where the stucco is falling away to show brick
has become a favorite place—my dog likes it.
I like it, too, and think of it as Italian,
crumbling like the empty Vicenza villa
Palladio built for the lizards to whom its fissures
are the point of the wall. Il Grande's crest should show
a lizard, couchant, rere regardant. Decay
is only offensive to arrivistes and tourists.

20.

A thaw, and the curbside walls of granite gray
snow melt; there is a general pardon,
unexpected, as for the king's daughter's marriage.
The corner guard-towers shrivel to puddles
the sun glints on. Pallid as felons, we blink
in the glare of a moment we hadn't allowed ourselves
even to think about, arrived at last.
Like a boy, I'm outside in shirtsleeves, only to learn
what boys have to learn, and men to remember:
that snow's melt means mud, and if the white
mess turns to black mess, mess remains constant.
Half a block, and I pick my steps like a geezer.

21.

The sky, on a clear night, lights up like a switchboard.
In the country, they see even better, where professors
trek in Land Rovers over rutted tracks
to profit from wilderness. Here, the light pollution
blots out tertiary stars—as indeed it should.
Let them compete, like actresses, like tenors,
for our dulled attention, shining in the city
skies or not at all. We've plenty of lights,
but the spaces between that made Pascal go giddy
dare us like unfamiliar alleys where footfalls
echo in menace and darkness comes alive
as it did for us, to us, when we were children.

22.

The city's bubble of light becomes, a party,
a fête, a *gin dansant de minuit à l'aube*.
"You gin?" "One gin," says Pushkin behind the bar.
It was Nabokov's joke. From such distractions
our skies glow. Our neighbor kept a few chickens;
his rooster crowed all night, deceived by that glow
that ought to have been the sun. By dawn, exhausted,
his patience and hope wasted, he'd fallen silent.
Dumb bird! Still, these tricks of the light
mean something. Through Sister Selena's window,
the red of the Don't Walk sign washes the faces
of her importunates, telling her their answers.

23.

The black relents—or seems to (knowing better
doesn't destroy the illusion), and light in the east
draws them to the beaches, revelers, tourists,
even some of the locals, to walk the clean
strip of sand the water has left swept
smooth as what they long for. Come, amigo,
rest here under the palm and watch. See?
They all do the same thing, the same way,
kneel or bow to take off their shoes, walk
to feel the cool smoothness under their soles,
and then they wade, wash their feet. Relenting
is what they crave in what is left of a rite.

24.

On the Kona coast, beyond the old royal enclosure,
on a spit of land cut off by a high wall
from where the fat kings trod, is the City of Refuge,
bare black lava rocks, an occasional palm,
a few tidal pools, and nothing, nothing . . .
The sea's emptiness, the sky's vacuity,
and the rocks' bareness meet on that narrow point
where sinners came, cowards fled from battle,
or the vanquished scurried for forgiveness, safety,
and cleansing. I've stood there, trying its magic,
but can't tell. Maybe I should have stayed longer
to let the emptiness work. Nothing helps.

25.

Behind the taboos was fear, the ground under
their feet treacherous, volcanos peaking above
sea level, and Pele, the goddess of craters,
boiling in rage. Their own natures were cheerful,
content with only seven consonants,
the blocks of their nursery culture (and thirty-nine
different words for *lazy*). Earth tantrums
and sea storms are infantile, dramatic,
but kid stuff: on the top of Kilauea
steam rises and sulphur, a big bully
menacing the playground. The Park Service
has marked the line we are not to try to cross.

26.

Or a drunk, maybe. Old George Lycurgus
who managed Volcano House back at the start,
in the '60s when it was two hard days on horseback
from Punalu'u, used to look at her seethe,
gaze out over the big caldera
and figure she needed something to settle her down.
When it got bad, he'd fling her a bottle of gin
which Pele loved as much as the pigs and dogs
the Hawaiians used to sacrifice. Why not?
She wasn't offended, probably liked a belt
as much as the next girl. So old George thought,
who knew her as well as anyone, nut that he was.

13

27.

The lava flow is whimsical, lines of force
self-correcting, variable. The liquid
possibilities harden to rock fact.
But here and there, as in history, kapukas—
islands in the disaster left by the quirk
of a diverging flow—survive untouched, cut
off from the rest of the field, the rest of the world,
five acres, or fifty, Lichtensteins.
As if nothing had happened, the flora continues, inbreeds,
turns weirdo. Such *anciens régimes*
figure our longest chances, deepest fears:
left to our own devices, somehow saved,
what caricatures of ourselves could we become?

28.

At ground level where all the dead birds fall to,
and sea level where all the dead fish rise to,
air, earth, and water meet at their borders
to collect each other's garbage. Heights and depths,
oscilloscope lines, exhaust themselves, collapse
to an even flatness, the silence of that thin green
swath of seaweed, the high tide line on the beach
I'm lying on, letting my brain poach
as I imagine balloons and bathyscaphes,
mountaineers, spelunkers, and feel the fatigue
of their strenuous efforts. I try to rouse myself
to trek ten yards to the snack bar for iced tea.

29.

To move is to seek an end, completion, fulfillment . . .
Therefore, only imperfection moves,
and only from what is at rest, content with itself
can we learn what we need to know. It will not tell us,
need not utter, utterly indifferent
to otherness, its itness perfect, enough.
The drunken sea staggers, trees flutter
nervous fronds in the air the birds wheel on,
but the black rock, smug at the end of the strand,
is just there, not even glinting in sunlight
or shining with wetness, dully itself, harder
than any of us can imagine with our soft heads.

30.

Il Conte says, "Nearer is larger." It's true
that Tibetans are tiny as mice, Australians, Brazilians,
cute dwarfs. Our parents, children, wives
loom larger than faces on Rushmore, blotting
the face of the sun as we do for our dogs
whose job it is to keep us from shrinking, balloons
with slow leaks. The doc's first questions—
height and weight—are always the toughest. I gorge
candy, potatoes, booze; my weight is still
problematical, my heart's big burden,
otherwise wispy. I cling to the leash to keep
from floating away to cold, giddy Tibet.

31.

The floors were lower then, and we climbed chairs
as Alpinists, to tame them, turn triumphant,
and wiggle our toes out over their ledges.
Giants walked the earth then, by whose obscure
magic food appeared, and toys, and we
were their toys, *i.e.* repositories
of imagination and love. But furniture shrinks,
houses shrivel, Rushmores dwindle down.
We find ourselves suddenly big, exposed
to weather's ravages, and tromp the earth's
uncertain crust. That floor, once nightmare distant,
nightmare fast rises nightmare near.

32.

The plants in Dr. Kronkheit's office thrive
from all the talk. He takes comfort in this
demonstration that therapy does some good.
"This fear of falling began when?" Begonias
attend, bask in my story. I take off the coat.
My father wouldn't/couldn't fly. His healers
were Smith and Dale. Kronkheit practiced in Cairo
(a Cairo practor) but his maxims help,
stupid as they are (all courage is).
In my ear, in my father's voice, they resound:
"You had it before? Now you have it again."
"It hurts when you do this? So, don't do this."

33.

Tough sayings, covering many cases,
among them *Delmore Schwartz* v. *Kramer,*
The City of New York, Nelson Rockefeller,
God, et alia. He was a second cousin
of my first wife's mother's cousin's husband. We
met once, and he complained—of course—
but seemed sane and badly used. I sent him
to see my father, who said he couldn't win.
They yelled. My father threw him out. An affront
to art? Schwartz loved cats. They kept running away.
From poetry? No, from disorder and ill-luck.
The cat sits on the mat. My luck holds.

34.

Cheaper than blackjack, as reliable as
tea leaves, biorhythms, or yarrow stalks,
I play solitaire, not to test my skill—
it needs none—but my state of grace, the world's
responsiveness, the cards' will, dumb
but as true as any trick of metonymy
Selena knows. A momentary stay
against confusion, Frost called a poem,
but (eight on the red nine) this can work too.
I cheat sometimes, but don't count those games.
It's only a way to show the cards the way.
They're slow to learn. The name of the game is patience.

35.

Patterns, intellectual expectations
blind us to the truth which is a jumble.
Late at night, in a strange city, lost,
trying to find one of the boulevards,
you turn a corner, smell bread baking, and feel
safe for the moment. The growing, milling, and baking
of grain is civilized and comforts. But that
isn't what you've stumbled on; it's mother's
kitchen, or grandma's, faraway cues
of old scenarios. You may get mugged,
or not. But emboldened now, you can persist
and may yet find the way back to your hotel.

36.

Charts are only approximate. Out there,
the sandbars shift, the meandering channels writhe
like live things. You learn to stare at the water's
changes of color, of surface, and guess where
to go with the wind on one cheek and a sense,
semiconscious, of the tide: you scan
the bay, hunch your course, getting the boat's
feel of the day, the wind and the water, afraid
always of screwing up. Waist-deep in water,
and ankle-deep in gull shit, hauling the boat
back to the channel, I've considered my failings
in attention. And humility. And tact.

37.

We lie to our children, try to persuade them to build
their characters up and lower their expectations,
preach to them stern words we've heard ourselves,
Sois sage et travaille bien. We hope
they will, and want for them glittering prizes
they'll earn while we watch. O, let the sun
glint on the oars, and let my daughter's shell
slide over the water like light—for me,
for the grace I had in me somewhere that she wears
like a bright sunhat. In the lottery
of the world's poor dream, she has my number.
The unearned are the only triumphs that count.

38.

Grit that seeps in under the window frames,
blackens the sills, and, despite my attacks with Kleenex
and an idea of order, accumulates,
expresses the right relation of subject and object,
underscoring the view, a cityscape
of which it is a part, brings outside in.
Any idea requires such grit, grist
to grow on and correct to. Dust in the air
swirled before the creation and crept in
to body the prime mover's first notion,
embarrassing the grandeur of intellection
with small domestic matters: matter: this.

39.

Not only darkling but dankling and damned bleakling
(if 1 may be plain—obnubilated), this
bare heath where the military, stupid—
it's never clever—skirmishes still . . . Hell!
Stoicism is heartless; passion useless;
madness beside the point: the starveling hordes,
huddled along the border, die by the thousands.
This is no hyperbolic figure but true,
awkwardly true, giving to all our actions
the gravity of indifference. Whatever we do
is in the face of that, in spite of that.
Even frivolity now must be in earnest.

40.

The picador horses around. The matador
does dumb tricks with his cape, veronicas,
betties, archies . . . It's the exterminador
I cheer for from my seat on the sombre side,
with his can, his pump, and the sweet smell of a death
I hope will be exquisite, lingering, and thorough.
But they'll be back, the roaches. "They don't like crowds,-
and want to spread out. To the suburbs," my affable killer
jokes and squirts the bathroom. Outside, sirens
wail. Illness? a fire? Or Coronel
Corrupcion's tireless, brutalizing,
brutalized men, reestablishing order.

41.

Sweating in their splendid gowns, they parade
a loop around the green and through Phelps Gate
to the Old Campus, one or two of my old
teachers among them still, and now my son.
Admissus est. And then we are stevedores,
lugging crates to the station wagon. None
of the snapshots catch this sweat, the freight of it,
the way he goes north with his mother in the wagon
and I go south, nor should they. Ceremony
is staged, posed, an art. Trumpets and banners
say all the important banal phrases for our
mute hearts. Tantantara. Tzing-boom!

42.

In the Café Royale, we imagine ourselves
rich and powerful; downstairs, in Vagine's,
the disco in the basement, we are gorgeous,
sexy in the noise and glittering lights
of the hot boîte; upstairs, in the green and gold
lobby, we may be gracious and indolent.
From the cues of these contrived obvious sets,
we may escape into town to walk the seedy
streets and browse their impromptu junk—a *salon
des refusés* El Jefe has contrived
to divert the exquisite or challenge the brave
few who do not own or belong. Or care.

43.

The ancient theories of vision with beams of sight
arising from the eyes and bouncing back,
like radar, in those old drawings are right:
we inform the world with bulldozer whims, impose
by our very observation a crude plan
on subtle topologies, tidy, and diminish—
which is why in the gardens of Versailles or the mad
boulevards of Paris or Washington
one succumbs to the hypnotist's trick languor.
In the railroad's slide-show, though, is a livelier jumble:
in that scrapyard, for example, a pile of bathtubs,
glinting, frisk like dolphins, freely themselves.

44.

Months later, languishing, its five
monstro leaves down to three, and two
of those now with the fatal brown at their outer
edges, the thing hangs on. Hangs on,
with suckers from outside the thick center
bulb I'd thought was dead, flooded out
or dried out, or the cat killed, sending smaller
shinier leaves the same monstro shape
up to the light. The lessons of *La Nature*
mean nothing. I decline its cheery
stupid hints. Still, we water again—
no doubt to kill with care what survived our neglect.

45.

Air shimmers and asphalt melts to goo
on the first hot day of the year. Windshields
and bumpers gleam like kitchen utensils where this
exotic dish, vindaloo curry or
Mongolian hot pot, seethes like the magma
into which we must all fall and dissolve
in a new geometry where points, lines,
planes and solids cook down, onions
in the soup du jour. The coronel observes
life may be a fountain, or maybe not.
Reality is easier. That's borscht.
His rule on a hot day is hot soup.

46.

The keen senses depend on waves in the air,
snares for the eyes and ears. The hands, slower,
grope to their certitudes, as the crude nose
and tongue diddle with samples of actual stuff.
The modest yield of their dark silent studies
we trust as the honest stammer of a dullard.
Hard/soft, sweet/bitter, hot/cold,
or excess—pain—or moderation's pleasure
are true enough and truly enough. Consider:
what blind fish in a cave pool know,
they know well. In the dark, I remember bedrooms,
where the bed was and where was the door.

47.

At tea on the verandah, we discuss
the day's events. Tea is an event,
and the little cakes are events. What did the paper
say of the elections? Of the market?
Or, more important, what is the menu tonight?
The weather tomorrow? Underneath the table
the poodle of Madame de Particule
hopes for scraps, his upturned cynic's eyes
following our conversation, dinner
and the heat subjects of interest to him, too.
What other subjects are there? From down the corniche
a sports car's engine makes a mosquito buzz.

48.

Late last night an alarm's mechanical keen
woke us. An automobile? A shop? The shrill
note extended itself for an hour, was sound,
then a sensation, then an idea of itself.
Someone called the police to inform them of trouble,
and later someone else called to complain
of the noise that had become the trouble, and then
somebody stopped it and all of us felt the silence
hatch glossy black from its egg of noise.
Speech was impossible, motion, out of the question.
With great strength, Madame, nevertheless,
bit into a peach and brought us back to life.

49.

That crazy people talk to themselves, narrate
their errands, say, in elevators, where we
are embarrassed and pretend not to hear, is not
surprising: which of us hasn't, under pressure,
suppressed or failed to suppress the mumbled phrases,
templates of syntax with their illusion
of reason and direction. Schoolboy assignments—
Latin, French, algebra, history, English—
bubble up in me still. And poets pretend
to that necessity, try to deserve that same
crazed attention, providing words to mutter
on the way to the laundry, post office, grocery, bank.

50.

Sick unto death with circles, revolutions
and orbits, horizons, the round eyes' arbitrary
limit to the whirling globe, I return,
bringing my children back to these old quadrangles'
rectitude where they may find respite
from dizziness in stones laid upon stones.
Outside, in our city's rubble, the few surviving
palazzos, settled out of true, stagger
the mind like strong drink. To remember the plans
is heartbreaking. O, but gentles! Not to remember
would be heartlessness. Marx brothers, we stand
looking ridiculous, holding up the walls.

51.

His policies didn't cover acts of God;
the company therefore could reject all claims,
countering with its own—that any event,
good, bad, large or small, was God's,
Whose eye was on the sparrow and their fine print.
Premiums? They were acts of faith, he explains,
propitiations, sacrifices. He fled,
hounded from the States by unbelievers
(that too was an act of God, as it was for El Jefe
an act of principle, dollars and Swiss francs,
to offer asylum: sanctuary much).
He plays bridge well, but overbids.

52.

"Whether clever or stupid, those beautiful young
men and women, bound for the tennis courts,
are surely ignorant, having suffered or lost
nothing." The coronel's point? That only torture,
whether from nature or human nature, elicits
truth and turns evasive minds to face
demanding questions. He calls his secret police
midwives to truth, regrets the labor pains,
shrugs, falls silent, stares at his shiny boots.
The refuge of our frivolous verandah,
precious, fragile as crystal, is permitted
as doctors permit their terminal patients dope.

53.

Charters, reprieves, commissions, pardons—El Jefe
sits at his desk, it's said, in the afternoons
and flies them as paper planes. Those few that make it
beyond the rosewood case for the constitution
he grants; he denies the rest. It's whimsical,
but all systems are. Why should the eloquent
and clever sell their skills to the powerful rich?
The poor, the inarticulate need protection.
So does the regime. Let handy children
prosper as *abogados*. Let losers blame
bad luck. Unless it's only a fiction
El Jefe suffers, indulging our delicate hopes.

54.

The articulation of matter, the reduction of all
that singing jumble to a formula,
and in that odd timbre, is the bassoonist's
art. A philosopher's right instrument,
the bassoon is witty, abstract, but still homey,
honking its verities of boop bah beep.
To understand the creator's principles,
listen to that, the ground, the apparently simple
equation on which the music rests as we
long to do. To relax,'Einstein fiddled,
but these are serious reeds on which, correctly,
the infant Moses, floating in peril, snags.

55.

A simple solution: we moved it from the hall
to the bay window. With more light it revived,
survives, putting out pointy shoots from which
its jungle leaves unfurl, sea-lettuce green
to grow darker, five now and two more
I can see coming. All problems should yield
to such straightforward cures—a change of light,
a new place. All night long, trucks
freighted with such hopes roar on our thruways,
hopeless, wrong, as my poor dumbbell bulldog,
years dead, who used to crouch, stalking
electrical outlets she took to be mouseholes.

56.

The direct route to the summer concerts leads
through slums where, outside tenements, the tenants
of their predicament (and ours) play cards on stoops
and keep an eye on their gaudy nigger cars,
those vehicles of bravado and antic passion.
The powerful insolence of powerlessness
passes us, reckless, left and right, drag-starting
at the lights. We close our windows, lock our doors.
There is nothing polite to say. Next time we'll go
a more sensible way, to spare our senses,
as gay and savage as any of theirs, the fearful
roar of dual carbs and the smell of rubber.

57.

It is a bad dogsbody that dogs me,
will not jump through my hoops, snaps and turns
savage—too predictably. Untrained,
they'll do that, but even the best of them bite,
forgetting years of pampering, petting. They smell
fear (we are all afraid) and our impatience
that would aim the swift kick. I don't blame it,
but, wary, feed, walk, groom it, take
compliments for it, and let it lie under my bed,
until the whim of its abrupt distemper
sends it into the air, fangs bared
for the delicate pulse of my exposed throat.

58.

A red sun, and the world's tongue cleaves
to the roof of the sky. The air is sickening, sick.
We are advised to avoid exertion. The city
shines, queerly carnelian, amethyst, garnet
in its malaise. My mouth, once decked with porcelain
and silver of young manhood, now shows gold
that mocks mere meat. The need is greater
now than when the Pharaohs first perceived it,
to find the right preserving essences.
The hotel is a tomb today, but fine
grit seeps in to cover the sills. With a frail
finger I can sign them with my initials.

59.

Their shirts proclaim their sneaker brands, saloons,
universities, radio stations, cute
or rude remarks—"Boogie" or "Amateur
Gynecologist"—or Mozart's face,
or a beer can, as if an identity
were no more an achievement but a hope
impossibly remote, as if no day began
with fresh linen and prayers that its sweat stains
be minimal, its blood stains be escaped
until that blessed commonplace moment at night
when I fling my soiled shirt into the hamper
musty with other shirts and sheets I've survived.

60.

Lust and greed, a lust for images
and greed for the concrete, are fundamental:
without these grubby traits, you'd think it would run
clear as a brook, but, no, it dries up, dies.
Disgust may serve for a time, their opposite,
but less well. Poets are drummers of goods
and tire at last. Therefore, the hotel,
a refuge for the bored, is a cleansing haven:
its frivolous conventional decor,
its silent corridors and identical rooms
soothe the glutted soul, as does the view
of mangrove, bay, ocean, and empty sky.

61.

Even the changes for better are bad, affronts
to accurate recall. Why else should I care
if there is a new seawall at the beach or a vacant
lot in my mind's map is developed now
and has a convenience store? My life is not
a series of landmarks, and even if I've lived here,
the town's profiteers have nothing to gain from that
or my rare appearances to scrutinize
what I hardly noticed then. A visit's no good:
what the arrangement of stores, houses, trees,
and vistas meant, they don't mean now. At the house
the juniper's too high. I may not trim it.

62.

Monsieur Hubert, *chef de cuisine, artiste,*
is rumored to be a killer, to have fled
France, to have been given asylum here
for the tourists and for us. How else explain
a man like that in a place like this? The truth
is simply that he drinks. And Robert, the *maître
d'hôtel* is the murderer. But that delicious *frisson*
the patrons feel in the dining room for the chef,
invisible in back, would be *de trop*
if the truth were known and seen. Truth? In cooking?
It's a faddist taste, like vegetarianism.
Refined palates require more delicate fare.

63.

The chairs, the tables, even the brass floor lamps
out on the verandah are bolted down—
to discourage the thefts poverty prompts? No,
for our sakes, who have lost our mansions, groves,
and estates in one revolution or another.
My daughter's visit, for instance: three days
out of the summer's hundred. Not enough.
And the doctor's report to my father was not good.
Neither is my fault, but I blame myself.
I should have loved them more, shown it more.
From a chair, bolted down in the same place
reliably, day after day, I take much comfort.

64.

That the random pattern of rocks assumes, from this view,
the configuration of a plausible head, that
of an alligator or a crocodile, in profile,
says nothing at all of the rocks, the bay, the ocean,
but of perspective, fancy, and one's need
in the absence of any truth whatever—the rocks
are stubbornly rocks—to try to invent something
that may hold through the wicked lick of the night's tongues
and its savage baying till dawn reveal a snout,
hump, brow, and a neck's declivity
to tell me I'm still in the same place, awash
in the foam of churned vision, but still afloat.

65.

The tourists' improbable appetite for owls,
cats, raffia, macramé, copper, and seashells
strung into bracelets and necklaces is a craving,
poignantly silly but still all they can muster,
to hang onto something; they cram their luggage full
of times and places, knickknacks and snapshots
that will keep in some corner longer than the richer
subtler treasures—how the wind from the sea
slants the trees one way, or how a cloud
of fog spills over the ridge of the coastal mountains . . .
Memory fails, eye dulls, and the soul dulls:
knowing their limitations, they shop for their lives.

66.

Down toward Prunedale, before you cut west
to Monterey, there's a valley of onions, miles
of the smell of onions, too strong to be pleasant
but not awful. Odd. And you ask yourself,
what's it like to live there? Do they still
smell it at all? Our noses are nearly useless
except for tasting, for keeping our glasses on,
and to cover that awful hole in the skull. Smells
fade as the nostrils' primitive twitch exhausts . . .
But an ocean of onions! They visit San José
or San Francisco, reeking of them, I'd guess,
and not knowing: Sirs, the human condition.

67.

That she is lithe and agile as I am not,
with claws between the pads of her silent paws,
and is a killer matters—all desperado
gangs include such graceful diminutive types,
soft spoken, with a preference for the knife
or the garotte . . . They are pets too,
flatter the boss, whose power includes their powers,
just by hanging around. Thus, the cat
on my lap, athletic, whimsically savage, pleases,
supplies me with those jungle knacks I barely
remember how to desire—but seeing her pounce,
my hackles rise, and the beast in me hisses, "Yes!"

68.

Here in the lobby, the chandeliers' lavish,
if democratically random, glints enrich
sofa, escritoire, the mahogany table
with its relatively recent magazines,
and, of course, the guests, their pecking order suspended.
It's bedrooms that sort us out again. At night,
in the wee hours, insomnia or a cough
keeping us awake, the floor, the square feet,
and the windows tell us our worth, from the grande luxe
ocean views to the meanest airshaft gloom,
until the eyes close to a mercy of darkness
as evenhanded as the lobby's light.

69.

The electrical system is quirky. Power always
depends upon technology which has
its limitations, as all thought does—no one
believes in it any more, except the splinter
left, idealists, students (three different labels
for the same handful?). Elevators, lights,
refrigerators fail, and there's a buffet
of what would spoil, sumptuous, candle lit,
delighting our reactionary tastes.
It's not the end of the world but, say, the fun
of the end of the world. And then the lights come on,
radios blare, and we reset our clocks.

70.

Under a watery sky, on a high bluff,
a cow grazes. Beyond, to the left, is a farmhouse
with a kitchen garden behind it—cabbage, tomatoes.
The land falls away; a rail fence
keeps the cow, the house, the field itself
from falling into the sea. But what I see
is what I am: my eyes, on their stalks of nerves,
blossom with images I expect, blink
at what I cannot comprehend. Hubert
sees the same cow, salt, cabbage, tomatoes,
but knows more than I do, glimpses purpose,
possibility, destiny's kettle—soup.

71.

To let us suppose we know more than we know,
to arouse our expectations, play on them,
and with a small surprise fulfill them, paying
a compliment to our shrewdness, shrewd musicians,
like novelists and playwrights, stack their decks
to deal us winning hands. Their last notes fade,
and we are in love with ourselves, giddy with wisdom,
or what it would feel like to be wise. We aren't
better or different, cannot manage our lives,
with any particular grace, or even, next morning,
watching a pigeon swoop through the grit of the real
sky, predict the spot where it's likely to land.

72.

In even the best hotels, the carpets stop,
and behind the swinging leather-covered doors,
the floors are tile or cement, and the illusions,
quite reversed, as if the establishment were
a factory or a warehouse, those bare bulbs
shining on the no-nonsense tile walls
of pantries, kitchens, work rooms, and corridors
in the perfect clarity of hospitals, prisons,
and morgues. Every so often, I like to visit,
pretend some errand, and smell the disinfectant
soap they use on the floors—for the vertigo
of seeing into the future, looking down.

73.

A swirl of autumn leaves, and the dog goes crazy,
darts, snaps, pounces, catches, caught
in the faint twitch of an old instinct, as we
thrill to see, in the gallery's back room,
a shrunken head. Authentic? *Mais, bien sûr*!
The price is cruel enough, and someone will buy,
who delights to imagine himself in the rain forest,
blowgun at his lips, eyes peeled, ears sharp,
his breath shallow . . . or hates it, fears its ugly
blandishments: simplicity, directness.
One needs some poise to look from this wizened face
to that of the sleek dealer. *Merci, non.*

74.

To dance outside of my house, yes, to dance
that *aktive Vergeszlichkeit* . . . that is to be
free, as a pot is free, an old pot,
blackened with its years of feasts, but empty
for a child to use as a pail, wear as a helmet,
or bang as a drum, that it, too, can play,
its old stews long ago eaten
or dumped. I must be that gay child, that pot
ringing in my pudgy hands and meaning
nothing more or less than I mean it to mean,
for soon enough, I shall be recalled
to the measure of rooms, their purposes and decorum.

75.

The crossed out word calls out; I hold the paper
up to the light to catch its eloquent muffled
meaning, to reconstruct, as a curator might,
what is lost, stillborn or murdered. A clean page
lies, implies an impossible Eden, nothing,
not even a single leaf, dead on the greensward.
It cannot be. Great beasts have thrashed in the tarpits;
their names are crossed out words. Armies have perished
in blinding snows. What these survivors say
is never the whole story. What did you mean,
or ought you have meant? On flimsy onion skin,
the letters writhe in the light and our discomfort.

76.

In the hills, they say, is a tribe so primitive,
they use metal washers for coins. The boys
every so often talk of an expedition
to rob them blind: a few bagsful of washers,
and one could buy the whole damned village. At night,
when the bar is quiet, they think about it. Yes,
and decide to go—next week, tomorrow morning.
But what's up there to steal? What have they got
worth the trip and the hauling back down?
"Poverty as a defense," the professor proposes,
but nobody laughs. It's an intellectual trick.
The intellectual trick. Ours.

77.

Roses here in the tropics riot, bloom
themselves to death in an orgy of growth, put out
like mad, exhausting themselves, huge tired
flowers with almost no scent, then nothing.
The management flies in fresh replacements,
and at night workmen dig out the old, stick in
the new. Down the hill, in the rows of brothels,
the same horticultural rules hold,
with new faces appearing to put on the old
rouge, until the bush wilts. Fans
turn overhead like lazy prayer wheels, as we
crane our necks and try to imagine cold.

78.

It rains every afternoon at four o'clock,
a pelting rain, the water drops like metal,
bouncing like rivets, like bullets, off the blacktop.
Palm fronds wave the arms of surrendering troops,
but there's no relenting. Rivulets on the pane
converge in the tracks of brigades in rough terrain.
Or, worse, it is the weeping of a child
beyond the recollection of his cause;
his wracking sobs are stones he gasps around.
I cannot remember, but I must have cried
that violently once. How else can I watch now,
knowing the exhausted calm it will come to?

79.

That El Jefe is dead is likely. As good as dead
is sure. Shot, poisoned, or stabbed in the formal
Roman fashion? Or simply shut away
in some asylum? The papers report only
the pleasure of the regime, which is now the brokers,
doing a deal that does not much concern us,
for what can we hope for better or worse? Here
is no Sarajevo. No aspirations seethe
to turn the lush landscape into a bloodbath
of consequence. No better than the dead,
a new Jefe will stare from ubiquitous posters
to fill the same blank spaces on peeling walls.

80.

Small arms fire at night. The lure of disorder
brings campesinos down from the hills to loot,
grab what they can, and glean, and soldiers to shoot.
Or perhaps the soldiers, themselves, are looting and fire
only at fictive malefactors who hover
directly overhead where they aim. The charade
is well rehearsed and safe enough: a few,
no more than at a soccer match, may die,
but our roads are bad and our traffic fatalities, rare.
Here at the hotel, where the mistresses
of several Excellencies are ensconced,
we have their gauzy peignoirs for our armour.

81.

Our delicate stomachs and unreliable guts
know better. The chef therefore connives
with the *présentation*—with flaming sauces,
ice sculptures, simulacra in marzipan—
to woo the children in us who will wolf
whatever is set before us. *Mes enfants,*
let us pretend we are hungry. Have a forkful!
The waiters are like zookeepers who pamper
their specimens of endangered, expensive species,
shoveling into their cages tidbits to tempt
the incurious strange beasts we gawk at, totems
of our blocks and coloring books, our oldest friends.

82.

The curfew has lasted a week: we become accustomed
to life in a children's city where only the naughty
are roaming the dark streets, playing the savage
games we all recall. The ground rumbles
when a heavy tank grinds by. (There are only three
or four and the soldiers have to take their turns
playing at tank; the toys are always the same
and never enough.) We're either being punished
for some forgotten mischief, or we are sick,
recovering, our fevers broken. Our dreams
rage outside. In the national palace, grown-ups
converse in those low tones one can never quite hear.

83.

The dignity of politics? The coronel
produces a very expensive fountain pen
from somewhere in his tunic, holds it up,
and asks what it can do. "A doctor, a judge,
or a general can kill with it, but a dentist
is a figure of fun because he seldom risks
his patients' lives. In times of peace and plenty,
politics also is trivial, but now . . ."
He unscrews the cap, stares at the broad gold nib,
and with a lethal flourish signs his bar chit.
"The crocodile, most of the time, is sleeping,
but when he wakes, there is sudden beautiful silence."

84.

From nowhere, abruptly filling a leaden sky,
a flock of birds wheels through the air, turns,
rises, passes a tree, and disappears
over a hill off to the left. What?
What does it mean? To a mosquito, fear;
to a cat, the thrill that freezes its lithe body
to a still ravening shadow; to some men,
an itch of the trigger finger. Uninvolved,
I can consider their grace, their irrelevant beauty
(up close, a single bird is ugly
and probably mite-ridden). Like that tree,
I think I have had a brainstorm and am wrong.

85.

Chambermaids, bellmen, busboys disappear,
possibly jailed or killed, or just afraid
of being jailed or killed. We have buffets;
there's no room service; no one turns down our beds.
I miss those little mint wafers in green foil
they used to leave on the pillow. Last night there was thunder—
we hoped it was thunder, but it could have been a
    bombardment.
The bar stayed open late. Someone played the piano,
and the rest of us sang, mostly college songs
from Princeton, Yale, or Notre Dame. Why not?
We had forgotten, or never learned in the first place,
the hymns we were nearly frightened enough to need.

86.

The times are peculiar: if they are not peculiar,
then they are peculiar. Such paradoxes
are soothing, expressing as they do our shrill
unease. The abundant empty moment
is tolerable enough. The sun strews
the wet grass with its worthless diamonds, and birds
sing in the trees, their rich ungenerous gift
decking the morning, but newsprint blackens our hands
with yesterday and tomorrow, five minutes ago
and five minutes from now, their pains, their risks.
At breakfast, on the patio, flatware gleams
like the bayonets down by the main gate.

87.

The laundries have ceased to function. Our clothes, our lives
are rumpled now, still mostly clean (we can wash
underwear in our sinks) but never ironed.
Our delicate conceits wilt in the heat.
We all look awful, except for the coronel,
immaculate in authoritative khaki,
and the monsignor in a soutane nuns have pressed.
The Junta already has the radio station
and the newspapers . . . But laundries? Well-turned-out
boys in school were often the bright ones. The army
must have new uniforms—by St. Laurent
or Hardy Amies—to stabilize the regime.

88.

Those pastel rectangles were living rooms once,
and their theoretical spaces windblown birds
fly through were discrete, closed. The building
was torn down or it fell, and the painted places
catch the afternoon sun as they never before
could. Like seashells we pick up on the beach
at the high-tide line, they are smooth, burnished by flesh
they once held, and gaudy. What maniacs
could have chosen such lurid greens, livid yellows
to live in and with? Only trivial ghosts
could haunt those airy flats; serious spirits
hang back a while to wait for the paint to weather.

89.

A new Jefe—a figurehead of course,
for the portrait for stamps, notes, classroom walls
and official bureaus. The weakest of the lot,
but if he is shrewd and patient, he'll grow stronger
as the others knock each other off, grabbing
money and power in varying proportions,
for all the time, those two eyes, lithographed
a hundred thousandfold, will watch what they seem
to watch, approving, condemning, and hypnotize
the pretense real, and finally even themselves
to forget the cautionary vivid picture
of the old Jefe, lying in all that blood.

90.

Sacks of old mail are getting delivered,
and all of us in the hotel are recalled
like Lazarus to life by our old checks,
old bills, and old news: reports
from our children's schools, word of the deaths of friends
we never knew were ill, announcements of sales
already held, cruises missed, and concerts
long silent . . . The large question recedes—
whether we shall survive the week, the month—
and we are reduced to our smaller familiar concerns.
It's what they wanted. Someone shrewd decided
we might safely distract ourselves with our lives.

91.

These gifts have never been adequate to meet
the demands I make on them, infer from them . . .
But even that increase of talent, of mastery
for which I have groused and prayed, would keep the same
imbalance, the yearning for more, the same or more.
The carpenter, tinsmith, potter are not so beset
but in their materials happy. I envy them
their smells and noises, but most of all their showers
that wash away good sweat. Then they get drunk
and fall asleep. Fancies, drunken rages,
and dreams are my stock in trade, nothing, nothing
to airy thinness beat. It won't wash.

92.

The representations of gods—longevity,
prosperity, and posterity—emerge,
strutting their stuff for their real counterparts.
The merely human audience overhears.
All Chinese opera starts with these questions
dancing round in everyone's mind, dancing
across the stage like Larry, Moe, and Shemp,
loonies who may keep the good times rolling
right along or poke you right in your eye.
The action proceeds. I try, as all of us must,
not to be too much concerned for my father's,
my bank account's, or my children's sakes—those gods.

93.

There is no twilight here, but darkness whelms
suddenly from the east and the light flees,
leaving a bloodied rear guard holding the field
a few dramatic minutes. Then black.
Peepers take over and crickets; the whole palmetto
scrub and the jungle beyond it warbles the license
of night to feed and breed. Inside the hotel,
napery, crystal, and flatware gleam. A rose
dots each table. The jewelry, the gowns . . .
But having put on our brief show, we run
to rip those clothes off, burrow into the dark,
and make, if we're lucky, those very night noises.

94.

You search your pockets, wallet, begin to panic,
go through pockets again, feeling a fool,
and realize you've lost . . . How much? Forty dollars?
for which the bargaining starts. Having paid a price,
you appeal to your primitive sense of equity,
foxhole religion, figure you must have averted
worse disasters, that the evil, fickle gods
will move on now to some more amusing victim,
or you count your blessings for which this is a small
price to pay. And feel a worse fool
until forgetfulness, that profligate sport,
settles in easy indifference your account.

95.

Senor Martinez-Martinez, the big banana
of the Inca Finca, celebrates the birthday
of Carmen Miranda every year: he gives
a small dinner (for sixty), shows one of her films,
and makes his usual speech—to urge that her day
be made a national holiday—concluding,
"Vulgar as she was, so we are vulgar."
And he drinks to her energy, her extravagance
of hats mounded with fruit, those wonderful shoes,
those flashing eyes! He is, otherwise, sane,
takes nothing stronger than sherry, and in the evenings,
by the candlelight he prefers, reads Latin poets.

96.

In sewer trenches, grass is growing, for thieves
are thicker than blood or even sewage, and smarter
and dumber than we can imagine, who have lost all
ardor, outrage, everything but the trick
of being amused. The director of public works
seeded the excavations with artifacts
so archaeologists had to inspect each spadeful
of pre-Columbian dirt. But he used such cheap
fakes that the scholars are jailed, he's fled, and the trenches
still gape, while we wait for a new man, smart
enough to sign checks and contracts, but simple enough
to have that energy of belief we lack.

97.

A brilliant tinkle—Haydn or maybe Mozart—
floats down from the recessed ceiling speakers
of the doctor's waiting room. His magazines
dog-ear and, like his plants that turn brown, die,
but that apparently fragile but adamantine
andante will outlive us all, our pains,
their cures. Our grasp of that cadence that will not fade
loosens at last as, growing deaf, we imagine
silence. But no, men die, and that heartless music
without missing a beat will swirl through the air,
a gnat swarm glanced in twilight. One learns
like natives not even to try to whisk it away.

98.

The cows must be milked, of course, and the crops brought in,
and the medicine must be got through somehow by
sledge, outrigger, burro, by God . . . But the show?
Why must it go on? The troupers' golden
and only rule is silly enough to provoke
serious questions. Do they compensate
by their high moral tone for the frivolous lives
they know they lead? (They cannot all be so
stupid!) No, go back to drama as rite
when gods on the temple steps commanded performance:
then it makes sense. Now hospital aides
rent TVs to patients, a day at a time.

99.

Our childhood maps are accurate—a room,
a house, a yard with every shrub and tree,
even every branch distinct, remembered.
The town blurs a little to certain routes:
to school, for instance, counting the number of paces
on each block, or downtown to the movies,
the library, or my father's office. The rest?
It's triple-A and where the sun went down,
a guess I call a sense of direction. The road
is dark; its curves are dangerous, confusing.
The old maps are right. Go too far
and you risk falling off the edge of the world.

100.

A round number, a venerability:
if they were years, the television cameras
would grind as I gummed out a few words,
useless hints to the world eager to live
as long, longer, and show my telegram
from the White House. Nah! But turn them into pennies
with real heft now, which is to say
exchangeable for a child's first hoarded dollar.
It feels good. Great. I'm rich (would be,
if I could remember my first dollar). "Blesséd
art Thou, O Lord, who hast sustained me unto
this day . . ." I remember that.

101.

Useless? Yes. But harmful? Certainly less
than the churches with their bullshit, less than the banks
with theirs, the ministries and courts with their
piles of it high and deep, and less than the false
hospital hopes of those bright clanking machines
that extrude pain exquisitely. Here,
the offerings are limited but sane:
creature comforts at a price. With luck,
which is to say with money and health, the world
is yours to rent until that morning comes
when they throw you out and keep your luggage (but still
they wear white gloves and they call you "Sir").

102.

They claim to be on Fulbrights, claim to be
studying sociology and the theories
of Enfantin—who advocated clothing
that buttoned up the back, thereby reminding
its wearers of their mutual interdependence.
They have handed out hundreds of such garments
in the city's poorer neighborhoods, near the docks,
with illustrated leaflets of instruction.
Actually, they're here on Guggenheims
to study the aesthetics of practical jokes.
Each side, you see, would laugh at the other
except for their good manners—which are also a joke.

103.

As huge jets at touchdown whine regret
for the impertinence of flight and their violation
of natural order, trying to take it all
back in a loud apology and undo
by unsaying what has just been done,
so that our ears hurt from the vain negation,
so do our rales and rattles apologize
for the impudence of life, the organization
of proteins, tissues, organs, systems, into
this fragile elaboration which can't last
and doesn't. Common sense in the end takes over
and they're towed away, silent and contrite.

104.

Watches once were pets; with tiny keys,
or later with a crown-and-stem arrangement,
we fed them energy to chew to pieces
of time in a snug pocket. Later, self-winding,
they turned to parasites gobbling our gestures,
a frugal wheel hoarding all human movement
for its own to spend at a jeweled leisure. Observe!
Like hair, like the fingernails, it keeps on going
after the heart it mimics has failed, and the brain
it spoke to has tuned out. In the end, the watch
on the night stand tells us nothing in the stillness
of its hands of the stilled hand it used to pucker.

105.

The hotel has been sold. The bribes were hefty
and the price was amazing. The reason, nevertheless,
was anticommunism. The actual comfort
of some of the people ought not exceed the dreams,
the aspirations, the very imaginations
of most of the people. The international chain
will run the place down to acceptable levels—
for decorum's sake, as in the States, where beggars
all have dogs and pretend to be blind so we
may give for dog food and yet may not be seen,
uncomfortably too comfortable. Extremes,
hating each other, are drawn together like lovers.

106.

An endangered species like the whooping crane
or the bald eagle, they are shy and ungainly,
labor with their terrific wingspreads, and fly
to obscure promptings within their diminished haunts:
a handful of hotels, the yachts and flats
of a few friends. Their chateaux and estates
are all gone. Accountants fight to the death
and afterwards with taxmen, while they hover
in economic updrafts of pleistocene
biospheres like this. Not wicked, not
profound, they sail a tame sky like condors.
From here they go, perhaps, to the Costa Smeralda.

107.

Look at old Gomez run. He rings his bell
for garbage to be set out, and a block behind
the truck whines and gobbles, while burlier younger
garbagemen hustle on Gomez's heels. If he drops,
one of them will get his easier job,
which anyone would prefer. Gomez, himself,
used to run with the truck, banging the cans,
hurling the big bags, and hoping the man
with the bell would drop dead. And he dropped dead.
They all moved up, and Gomez got the bell
and the hatred, too. But he can save his breath,
needing no worse curse than the bell he rings.

108.

The airline posters and travel bureau brochures,
crude as vaudeville hookers, offer Paris,
London, Rome . . . a tower, a bridge, an arena,
glyphs which the places themselves aspire to
or dwindle to, as only paradise
properly should. Where is that curve of beach
with the palm in the middle distance to stand for all
islands, and whose is that curve of golden thigh?
A moron would remember more precisely,
but (check my gaudy sportshirts through) I can't.
Poster flat, I shall lie on that beach and think
of myself here imagining being there.

109.

The rocks and wrecks are terrified too and skitter
through all that black and wet with the very panic
we'd feel ourselves to huddle together under
the nursery jangle of buoy bells or bask
in the beam's reach. No, I tell a lie.
It's the other way around: the egg comes second.
At sea, a blunder's at least as bad as a crime.
Each new wreck turns hazard beneath
the smirk-smooth reasonable-looking water.
Figure an unclaimed warning, some spot marked
always and only for you: do you dive or not?
You may kiss my torpedo, Gridley; Hardy's fired.

110.

The hotel recedes, becomes a bracelet charm,
a souvenir of itself I can squint into focus.
Solid or only plate? But time will tell,
for Fabergé was right about crucial scenes
of a life being trinket-tiny. The blur
of tears that keeps me from picking out my room
he froze to crystal, lapis, malachite,
appropriately enough. In all the ore
of any operation, value glints
at the rock-hard heart of which he liked to carve
some posed banal moment I can imagine
flashing before my eyes just as I drown.

111.

The stripes on the barber pole appear to arise
from the fixed base to writhe up toward the globe
as the marquee lights only seem to hurry
inward toward the theater lobby to show
what we should do. We're able to see through
our eyes' lies if we want, but the child in us
prefers not to, conspires with the crude
neon arrows pretending to be one moving
arrow staggering from Zeno's taut bow
across the Hogan's Heroes sign. Eat!
Our blinks ease it along, as if we were all
jailers, on watch but also on the take.

112.

If, as the French supposed, the English fogs
gave rise to a passion for action, morose thoughts,
and ardent broodings, while their own limpid
lucid air produced a bent for abstraction,
hypotaxis, analysis, and wit,
what follows from these lights? The fluorescent's
blue-white wash, its shimmer and faint buzz
gives war games, cybernetics, subatomic
nuclear physics, pallor, and *mal aux nerfs*.
The incandescent light we have seen, shining
in the eyes of rabbits—frozen by it, unable
to choose which darkness to leap to, hit.

113.

That which is strange, the bulbous chimney pots,
the blue tiles set in the walls, the full
skirts of the peasant women in green or red
or garish purple fades pastel, shrinks
familiar, dusts as the lazy eye wanders,
wavers from the effort of focusing
and the mind wraps itself in a cheap quilt
of ideas. Only now, departing,
we see what we should have seen, all along,
in the febrile clarity of a reddish dusk
and remember the gold of sunrise and the diamond
glint of promises no noon could fulfill.

114.

The corniest gesture finds its necessary
moment as the crude truth blooms to a gaudy
flower no child with her colored tissues
would dare construct. The baritone cries out;
the tenor's a fool; the basso's a knave; and they all
group around the doomed dumb soprano
to bellow our actual pain, to sing what we
would say if only we could, if the channels of feeling
were not silted up. You must understand
it's a desperate gamble only love or honor
could drive us to consider. "Capisco? Andiamo.
Coraggio!" I mutter over and over.

115.

Herman baby, life is short. *"Hermanos,*
bebe," is somewhat cavalierly rendered,
but the rest is close enough, in the light of which
the cavaliers have as much right to be heard
as anyone else. *"Que la vida est*
breve?" You bet! And lose in the long run,
no run being long enough. The motto
winds its way around the lip of the wine jug.
Herman sometimes has nightmares of waking up
stone cold sober that scare him silly—
in a dry county in Arkansas, where no one
even knows the words: "Brother, drink."

116.

"The roots in good order, the trunk, the branches,
leaves and fruit will be in good order."
Thus from the Master Kung, if we can trust
The Great Learning, but even without a source
seductive, for which of us would not if he could
"regulate his household, cultivate
his person, rectify his mind, make
his intention sincere, extend his understanding . . ."
But that makes any flaw a fundamental
fault, the weight of which must crack trees'
lumber, or mind's mettle. All under
heaven hangs on a thread of perfection? Snip!

117.

"Give me a place to stand," Archimedes said,
"and I can move the world." A smart-assed notion,
for what he wanted was someplace out of the world,
someplace else, just to admit which
would be to move the world a lot, a fourth
dimension, heaven . . . To hell with it! Give me
a place to lie down, and I can ignore the world,
not to say dream a better one, easy. The huge
lever he imagined could never have moved
the planet a millimeter closer to perfect,
but that hypothetical platform, that other place
invites our heavy feet, calling us still.

118.

Rapacity, as when the garage hikes rates
another seven dollars a month, will bring
the city down to its last defense: robbed,
I must turn thief to get back my fair share.
What choice is there? Park on the street where vandals
can reduce an automobile to fine white powder?
Pushed beyond their talents, men turn vicious,
rob and kill, or kill themselves, or mope,
unable to decide. The pressure molds us,
breaks us . . . We must get away. The sirens
beckon us to white sand beaches and blue
water from their blue and white cop cars.

119.

The feel of the smooth skillet handle, the dull
well-seasoned cast-iron black,
a velvet that turns satiny with oil,
and then that plainsong of frying onions: heaven's
hosts are unlikely to like those great twee harps,
but some such modest familiar instrument? Yes,
massed skillets, and the purr of eggs in the oil,
or the tessatura of beef browning. Listen:
if the wind is right and the traffic pauses, if
the weather is right, balmy enough for windows
to open like hearts in springtime, you can hear
hymns of praise from skillets everywhere.

120.

A black man with a joss stick in a clip
on his curbside stand hawks his ideas of hats—
not my idea, of course, or your idea,
but his, of what they might like, assuming
as he does a *they*, who, wraithlike, arise
as if from the sickening sweet smoke of the burning
incense stick. Every day, he lolls
and they appear to purchase berets, caps,
pastel morels, or *cèpes, outrés chapeaux*
in such taste as to make a case for starving.
But he thrives, they thrive, and the sandalwood cloy
for some minutes clings to our decent clothes.

121.

Offshore on the sandspit, vulnerable
to the wind's whim and water's random tantrums,
men who do not mind or cannot imagine
getting wiped out build summer houses, substantial
uninsurable structures, poised on the dune's
quavering lip, July's and August's toys
disaster will sweep away. Down near the inlet,
fishermen gleaning lumber from the wreckage
will put up impromptu shacks. It will again
begin as memory fades and nerve grows vivid:
even in the securest parts of Nebraska
nobody lives forever, right? Plunge!

122.

Even a dumb horse knows that what whips
do to the air, they can do to flesh. The trick
is less in the snap of the wrist than in the mind,
the horse's mind, in which that selfsame ring
glitters in harsher light and the same ringmaster
wears his rehearsal sweatshirt and blue jeans,
wielding a knout that reaches out to renew
the old connections of its nerve with his nerve.
Thus, by association, imagination
horses around and tames us all, for who
is enviably stupid (not to say brave)
enough not to snap to chivalric attention?

123.

What does the record record? The composer's idea,
the performers' and the engineer's. The coughs
of an actual audience, that airy batter
in which the notes sizzle a little is gone
as the broken hairs on three of the four bows
and the sweat on four faces from heat and fear
(even the best of them fear) are all gone.
But the adventitious appears, the fortuitous
hides itself inside the glossy sleeve
in dust, scratches, departures from the pressed
virgin sound that the diamond gnaws down
to irrecusable haecceity.

124.

The space beyond the horizon is much the same
as this space. But farther enough away?
It ought to be different, day for our night, summer
for winter, whatever the fanciful mapmakers
doodle in, imagining weird birds,
animals, plants, tribes, capriciously other,
to fear or yearn for. What could stout Balboa
& Co. find, rare enough to be worth
that long haul but completions and connections?
Below the equator, around the world from here,
my Doppelganger, or opposite (Oppelganger)
is happy and clever when I am stupidly sad.

125.

Frayed, scuffed, worn . . . What helped you once
dream yourself new as the shoes you stepped into
or the shirt you unpinned, unbuttoned, and put on
still stiff with its sizing, disintegrates
to the commonplace, descends faster than you do
to affront you at the end, when you throw it away,
or ahead and hate it for its clear glimpse of your
own career. *And who will fill your shoes?*
You know damned well they'll be given away
to the Sally-Ann to pass out to some bum
passing out on muscatel. The heels
you treed every night his stagger will tromp down.

126.

The Brownian swarms, of gnats, say, in the sunlight,
reduce us to esquimaux for whom the only
numbers are *one* and *two* and then *many*
or Greeks for whom ten thousand was countlessness.
The eye leaps to fly with the gnats, dive
and dart as one of them, chooses, loses, chooses
again, and closes, anxious. Flights of birds,
schools of speckled fish in their element
pattern a life you have lost but remember, uneasy,
facing into that sunlight, the screen of the lid
streaming crimson myriads, darters and swarmers
as thick as leaves, as profligate as stars . . .
You sit down to catch your balance, having seen
that anything you can count is never enough.

127.

It is late, the music loud, the ice gone,
the air thick, but the dancing goes on and on.
From a corner, I watch the provocative blouses open,
the provocative satin jeans tight, the oldest
person in the room. It had to happen
sooner or later, could have happened before
without my having noticed. Still, I should know
more than they do, having lived longer.
But it's less, I know less. I watch them writhe
in fun or cuddle together like puppies, sure
that the chair holding me cannot yawn for them,
nor the polished floor open to swallow them whole.

128.

That fussy façade is shrunk to postcard size
on the verso of a casual greeting: perspective's
storms buffet the old hotel, that huge
toy of a place. I remember a night flower
blooming the right moment and right place
to shift the entire scene, garden and wall
to hulking backdrop, when a chambermaid
—or whore, or probably both—before or after
her tryst was singing a song. Not to me.
I merely overheard how good it was.
She made the whole place hers till she fell silent
to let brute wealth and size reassert themselves.

129.

Friendship endures; love consumes itself.
It's obvious, trite. But who is not surprised
at the hatred our old loves bear us (or we them)
or struck by the similitude—that the taste
in the mouth is that of literal bitter ashes?
So with places: the generals' "scorched earth"
refers to those special places we can't return to.
Let it be that way for them, too. A beach,
a cityscape, a grove of trees were the holy
places we should have been content to die in,
had we been lucky enough. But we turned our backs,
and our guardian angels, weeping, bar the way.

130.

The action painters agreed—there is no background;
no place in the canvas is more important
than any other place; the tyrannical middle,
lording it over the corners for generations,
was only a pretender. In the remotest
province a couple of loonies plot together
and the capital trembles. In Key West, the conchs
reverse the order and try to imagine Hartford,
New Haven, and New York. And fail. The trick
is to see not with the mind's eye (vulgar),
nor the eye alone (stupid), but with great courage
with the eyes' mind, true blobs of the truth.

131.

As if the familiar feeling of the pen
in the cradle of the hand could help, as if
its ribbon of black on the paper could bind up
wounds or ravel a day that has come unstrung,
distracted, I take it up and put myself
in its care. It fails me and I fail.
But maybe a phrase I strike will sound solid.
Even the shoddiest walls have to have uprights
somewhere. Tapping, listening, tapping again,
and listening, I'll find them, solid enough
to bear weight, take a two-penny nail,
or even a spike about the size of this pen.

132.

It's all a fabrication. I confess,
my coronel, to having borne false witness:
the hotel, the city . . . Even the brown poodle,
asleep under the bed, is reinvented
every few months at seventeen bucks a clip,
and in turn he imagines himself in a cave lair,
deluding, deluded. Let's say the plant is real,
turning and reaching toward the one true sun.
In these gray cities' subtler latitudes,
the sun doesn't always show itself. What then?
Pale, perhaps sick, we invent a sun,
agree on one, face toward it all, and bask.

133.

They tell me the world is wobbling on its axis
and that the red shift means the universe
is flying apart. I know. What else is new?
The infinite spaces between the stars that scared
Pascal are even bigger now, the silences
even more silent. Giddy, I can't
catch enough of a breath to bid farewell
to my flown friends or, left alone, mourn
my lost illusions. Which of those sons of bitches
with whom I have drawn corks and broken bread
will show up at my funeral? Red dots
speeding away: I wobble, watching them go.

134.

In the Rue Borgne, the law winks where the fences
make wonderful neighbors and pawnshop windows offer
cameras, guitars, watches, rings, and handcuffs
to punctual, dandy, musical shutterbugs
with a taste for bondage. At local bloodbanks and bars,
the fluids ebb and flow in a way of life
like any other, until *monsieur le ministre*
opens the other eye to turn the raffish
poets, painters, models, musicians, and actors
into the riffraff they can seem, sensations'
darlings, offensive to you, the discerning public,
who do not have their nerves and lack their nerve.

135.

Childhood always looks better than it is,
seems to our inauthentic adult selves
authentic and spontaneous. It wasn't.
Some of the bullshit took us in; a lot
we saw but couldn't call—the word was forbidden.
Years passed and the rage subsided. Forgiveness?
Hell, no. A defect of recollection
and character: unable to face the truth,
we invent a happier time—then now,
and now then. It takes a grown-up's courage
to admit we were lucky to get delicate moments
too fine for our minds' coarse mesh to hold.

136.

As curs in the street bear witness, a few brusque
thrusts suffice; more than that is art
and beside the point, or what the stevedore
conceives to be the point, getting his load
into the dark hold. Perhaps perverse,
preferring distraction or needing illusion, we scorn
brute being to look to quality—
in the way a tendril of damp hair will sign
the linen's blank page. It never lasts;
that figure of impermanence proclaims
what good manners keep us from saying aloud,
but out in the plain air, the dogs bark it.

137.

The blowsy cabbage roses, the delicate fleurs
de lys, the iteration of trellis border
and scene can bemuse children or those under stress
(Raskolnikov considered in some detail
the condition of his wallpaper). The wall
behind it is solid enough, stolid; its thin
skin is what we agree on, what protects us
from barbarous plaster, brick, and hewn stone,
and the weather beyond and thieves. Whatever it seems,
it is, except for the seams that time will pick at
to tatter our fictions of civility—
an unpleasantness we can always paper over.

138.

The gardener planned a surfeit of green to ripen
a yearning in us for that *frisson* of pink
and set his flowering tree in its small thicket
to hide, shy, coy, to be surprised
as it signs the beginning of May. Though green and brown
try to reclaim the space, still that pinked nerve
throbs the rest of the year. As a big tongue,
doting, puzzled, flicks again and again
at the gap in its expectations, so I return
to rub my sockets clear with clumsy fists
and see what my certain pang says must be there
in that contrived glimpse through greenery's cleavage.

139.

The man overboard who swam for fourteen hours
to crawl at last onto some Trinidad beach
demonstrates indomitable spirit,
a lot of luck, or maybe the virtue of dumbness,
the inability even to imagine
not going on, taking the foreign fatal
breath of water and going down. The beach
in sight became—or should have become—boring,
obvious, certainly not worth fourteen hours
of pain and terror . . . The end glimmers in sight,
a wavering line I think I see, a joke,
a disappointment. Five more to go.

140.

The repetitive nature of nature—that this year's
leaves are like last year's—leaves the poor dullards
hope they may sooner or later learn it, get it.
(Got it? Good!) And all of us are dullards.
The lessons continue, as on a given day
in France where the *cinquième* is everywhere
identical, in theory the exact
same words spoken in unison
to produce a nation. So we study the lesson-
plans of these patient trees, their vivid new
leaves what we should have expected. I close my eyes
only a moment, and all goes blurry green.

141.

I cannot remember the wood I cleared, the sequence
of what bloomed first and what next, surprising
the way you surprise a baby with what he expects.
Peek-a-boo! The young are blind and the rich
are able to decorate up to their eyes. I
fall between, as better men have fallen
into the interior. The doctor
in Rutherford fell, the lawyer in Hartford fell
down through the pavement, up through the ceiling, odd . . .
But sight is odd that shimmers familiar cities
attractive, exotic. To be at home at home,
you need the lion tamer's whip and pistol.

142.

These pigeons survive where tough crows can't, dance
through traffic, beg, steal, crafty as gulls
or crude jays. The trick is seeing the sense
in pediment and cornice, merging with soot,
and being able to eat garbage, Twinkies,
kernels in horseshit. Most of us are awkward
seabirds that take a mile of ungainly running
to get ourselves airborne, and land hard.
Okay in the Keys or the Caribbean,
but not here. You got to learn street smarts.
Pay attention, birdbrain: know how to dart
down for sustenance, up for safety, and fast.

143.

The hewn stone is cool to my leaning forehead,
a prop, comfort, fortress, monument
all at once, and a caution—the stone wall
against which the apothegmatic head
bangs itself to a bloody pulp. But heads
perceived the rectangular solid, imagined the wall,
and gave the stone its shape and position here.
On an ordinary evening in New Haven
with my son and daughter, I am the ghostly presence
haunting them as my father haunts me.
I would fold them all in arms of stone and speak
in the stone's laconic tongue of reliable love;

144.

they don't believe it, as I didn't and don't,
but we can pretend, letting what faulty love
we bear one another pass for that best we deserve
to give and get. Those moments of courtesy
like dainty insects in amber could survive
as the data of history. Let grubby truth
be carted away—with New Haven, a grubby place
except in the mind. Drive on, and don't look back
to hobble imagination. Let our havens
always be new and the broken down world heal
as the poets have taught us to think it may. It may
if we say so often enough and loud enough.